MICHAEL BURRELL

The Man
Who Lost America
and
My Sister Next Door

AMBER LANE PRESS

First published in 1990 by
Amber Lane Press Ltd
Cheorl House
Church Street
Charlbury, Oxon OX7 3PR
Telephone: 0608 810024

Printed in Great Britain by
Bocardo Press Ltd., Didcot, Oxfordshire

ISBN 1 872868 00 2

The Man Who Lost America

CHARACTERS

THE OFFICER

THE RANKER

VOICE OF THE INTRUDER

The play is set on the ground floor of a cowshed which has living quarters above.

The place is Saratoga in the State of New York.

The time is November 1777.

The Man Who Lost America is in one act and lasts seventy-five minutes approximately.

The Man Who Lost America was first performed at the Chinook Theatre, Edmonton, Alberta on 21st August 1989. It was directed by Philip Grout with the following cast:

THE OFFICER: .... Michael Burrell
THE RANKER: .... Nicholas Moore
VOICE OF THE INTRUDER: .... Clive Swift

Sponsored by the British Council

The play was first presented in London at the Latchmere Theatre, Battersea on 4th June 1990, with the same cast and director.

FOREWORD

When I was a young actor I played General Burgoyne in a production of *The Devil's Disciple* given by members of the Royal Shakespeare Company directed by Ian Lindsay in the unusual setting of Wormwood Scrubs prison. It was an unforgettable night. We pulled in a bigger audience than the Billy Cotton Band, the previous biggest, and the atmosphere was sharply attentive and responsive and not a little charged by the fact that hanging, which features in the play, was a judicial sanction still on occasion carried out in the Scrubs. The reception at the end was rapturous. Though we did know about getting all the girls in the cast to stand in the front row at the call and bow very low.

And for me it began a continuing interest in and regard for the character of John Burgoyne. After all, there are not many generals who have a play running at Drury Lane while they are conducting battles on another continent.

Historians, even as recent as Hugh Brogan, generally treat Burgoyne as a failure who whinged, a tough if typical societal judgment on a man who lost a battle because, of the three armies that should have turned up to defend the Empire, his was the only one that did and was consequently at some disadvantage.

A little research among contemporary accounts (whether or not you include Burgoyne's own) discovers that Shaw's picture of the general as a humane, intelligent, witty and efficient officer is nearer the mark. How Shaw found time for his research in his own extraordinarily busy life, where most historians dont, is a separate marvel. Apart from my own eighteenth century reading I was greatly helped by Michael Glover's *General Burgoyne in Canada and America*, and the picture that emerged is of an urbane, caring, highly professional man whose career was sacrificed by his colleagues to save their own: it is significant that the Court Martial he sought was denied him. A Court Martial would have brought before the British public evidence of how his fellow generals in America and Ministers at home had played, or failed to play, their parts. The only inference is that they feared this. If the evidence would have condemned Burgoyne why did his peers strenuously avoid testing it in a court?

Now, in *The Devil's Disciple* Burgoyne is not the principal character and Shaw's splendid melodrama is more about the interchangeability of guns and bibles as the West's ideal way of achieving what it wants: warrior and missionary are kissin' cousins at the least.

In *The Man Who Lost America* Burgoyne is not merely central, he is in a sense the whole of the play as, say, Julius Caesar or Shakespeare's kings are in the plays that bear their names: they cast long shadows over the others in their orbit whose own problems to a degree stem from the eponymous character. This is certainly so in *The Man Who Lost America* though it allows me at the same time to provide (as one critic* has put it) "wry observations by both characters on military life, politicians, national characteristics and the human condition, matters unchanging down the centuries." I am entirely with Burgoyne's contemporary, Dr Johnson, that the particular should lead to some more universal view — without being too ponderous about it. And of course I have tipped my hat to GBS a few times along the way, as I should.

In another sense, however, the play is as much about the young soldier as it is about the general; it is about appearances, too, reality and deception. The young man's nakedness at the beginning is not just for effect. Though I had in mind a conversation with Peter Brook after he had seen the world premiere of the *Marat/Sade* in Germany, when he told me it started with a naked man leaping on to the stage, "a *coup de théâtre* from which the evening never recovered." I wanted to try the same device and see if I could recover the evening satisfactorily.

More importantly, though, *The Man Who Lost America* is about a relationship developing between two men who are apparently far apart in terms of authority, wealth, education and class: the one clothed in elegant finery, the other naked and probably afraid. Yet as matters transpire between them it is clear the youngster is the better survivor and with less to fear, and the differences between the men are nothing like as great as at first appeared. Literally Burgoyne restores the soldier's clothing to him; metaphorically each of them restores it to the other — so that the final decision they both take is to come out of hiding, to go up the ladder and to see what the world has to say — the very thing both were avoiding at the play's beginning.

Michael Burrell
Norfolk: January 1990

*Roger Diss, *Evening Echo*, 7 July 1989

THE MAN WHO LOST AMERICA

Burgoyne's hideaway as he prepares to leave America and face the music in England.

Some wooden boxes form a rough table and seat and other low boxes are pushed together as a bed on which straw-filled pillows and blankets are heaped. A muddied, worn Union flag hangs from the rafters. There is straw on the floor and a blanket covers an exterior window in the side wall. It is dark apart from the odd chinks of light. The sound of animals at their stalls can be heard through the other walls.

THE OFFICER, *well-dressed in shirt and neckerchief, breeches and knee-boots and wearing an elegant long waistcoat, comes down the rough wooden ladder at the back, visible by the light of his own candle lantern. He comes forward and looks round.*

OFFICER: It's not Drury Lane but it'll do. Indeed, I have seen actors in worse dressing-rooms. Perhaps this is a taste of the future.

[*He places the lantern where it sheds a little more light.*]
We negotiated with them as gentlemen. And as gentlemen we concluded an agreement. Then they broke it. Like gentlemen. They're the official enemy so it was on the cards. But what do you say to your official friends, who are always so much more vicious? Especially the ones you were at school with. God knows. I'll have to think of something.

[*He goes to the blanket over the window and releases it. A shaft of light breaks through, making the room much more visible though hardly bright.*]
The weather could be English: cold, motionless and not too bright. So. What to say, how to carry it off? It'll be the nail or the nosegay for my reputation. Bribery would probably work best, at least with my friends. Can't afford that. Shipwreck on the way home? It would be a solution, in every sense. With some appeal, Charlotte, you know that. But it lacks bottom and it wouldn't answer. Which leaves — a little wit, a little intelligence, a sharp memory and the truth. Tell 'em the truth, all of it. Yes, that should bring about the second great disaster of my career.

Friends at home are so fastidious. Everything must be filtered, whether it's sunlight or mulled wine or uncomfortable facts, passed through a sieve so that any grossness may be purged. Truth is so often so inconvenient.

[*He blows out the lantern.*]

It's the wits, then, and as much courage as I can muster. And deep preparation as always, so I shan't be taken by surprise.

[*He sits on the bed, then leaps up at a yell from beneath him.*]

Ah!

[*Jumping the other way, from under the heaped bedclothes, is a young man devoid of clothes.*]

Good heavens! My apologies, young sir. I trust I haven't interrupted you in the pursuit of your affairs?

RANKER: Don't do that again. You gave me as big a fright as a papist in an orange box.

OFFICER: I think it was mutual. Are you alone, or have you company under there?

RANKER: What are you talking about? Course I'm alone.

OFFICER: Ah. At a cursory glance you appear prepared for some sort of action and as a gentleman I wouldn't wish to intrude.

[THE RANKER *protects himself with his shirt which was his pillow.*]

RANKER: I've seen all the action I want.

OFFICER: Quite so. You are a soldier, I take it?

RANKER: [*uneasily*] What if I am?

OFFICER: Your uniform . . . it's a little unfamiliar, that's all.

RANKER: I can't help that.

[*He dons the shirt.*]

OFFICER: You must have an unusually parsimonious Colonel if that's all he'll dress his soldiers in. Or did you lose a rather heavy bet?

[THE OFFICER *sits.*]

RANKER: No.

OFFICER: I hope you didn't throw it away.

RANKER: You're an officer, aren't you?

OFFICER: Yes.

RANKER: I went in the river. It got wet.

OFFICER: It would have dried again.

RANKER: I think it probably has. You should know, sir.

OFFICER: I?

RANKER: You're sitting on it.
OFFICER: Upon my word.
     [THE OFFICER *rises and finds a stocking and a pair of breeches on the box where he had sat. He hands the stocking to the soldier.*]
     You appear to be short by one stocking.
     [THE RANKER *sits on the bed. He pretends to look around as he pulls the stocking on.*]
RANKER: It's somewhere about, sir. I'll find it.
     [THE OFFICER *hands him the breeches.*]
OFFICER: Your breeches.
     [THE RANKER *pulls on the breeches.* THE OFFICER *looks around without seeing whatever his eye is searching for.* THE RANKER *notices.*]
RANKER: It's probably here, in this lot.
OFFICER: What?
RANKER: The other hose.
OFFICER: Oh, that. Yes, I daresay. I can't see it elsewhere. I'm none the wiser as to your regiment. I take it you are an Englishman?
RANKER: Certainly I am. God, sir, you don't take me for a native, I hope?
OFFICER: That would be too harsh. Though their sartorial sense is sometimes similar. A few feathers around the head, maybe. How long have you been here?
RANKER: Since the campaign began, sir. Coming up to two years.
OFFICER: No, I meant here. This particular cowshed of Empire.
RANKER: Oh, last night. It was dark, I couldn't find my way.
OFFICER: From the river? That's a mile and more away.
RANKER: That was earlier. I was trying to get back to lines. Tired, soaking wet, you know how it is. And I lost my way and thought, here's a handy hole, let's get in here, keep out of the wind and the cold. Thought I could rest up a bit; then when it was light and I was dry I could find my way and present myself correct.
OFFICER: To whom?
RANKER: Beg pardon, sir?
OFFICER: Who would you present yourself to?
RANKER: The Adjutant, sir.
OFFICER: And what might his name be?
RANKER: Captain Tresillian, sir, since the battle at the farm. It used to be Major Hawkes. Till he stopped that artillery ball with his head.

OFFICER: So you're from the Ninth of Foot?

RANKER: Sir.

OFFICER: Not from one of the bateaux, or General Phillips' Artillery Park?

RANKER: No, sir, the Ninth.

OFFICER: How did you come to be in the river, then, so far from your lines?

RANKER: Well, I was looking for food.

OFFICER: Don't the rebels feed you? They feed me.

RANKER: Well, you're an officer, sir . . .

OFFICER: And as such I see that my men are fed. Since mid-October when they — and all of us — became prisoners, they've had no need to forage. American food may be tasteless and unimaginative but it has been more plentiful than His Majesty's dwindling supplies. In any case, how do you manage it? There are sentries posted, with no love for us.

RANKER: Like I said, it was dark. I gave them the slip in the dark.

OFFICER: Soldier, you said it was dark when you came out of the river. And because it was dark you were unable to find your regiment. If it was dark before, and you could find the river, you could find your way back. Or is my logic faulty?

RANKER: I wasn't sure. I was trying to find my way back when I spotted this . . .

OFFICER: Where's the food?

RANKER: I didn't get any.

OFFICER: Hardly surprising if you were trying to catch fish by hand.

RANKER: I was looking for a house, or some abandoned stores. Honest.

OFFICER: Or a dead man's haversack.

RANKER: Well, it wouldn't be any more use to him, would it? I only joined the Army because I was hungry. It's a good recruiting sergeant, an empty stomach and no prospects. And like most sergeants, it's not choosy about how it gets the results it's after.

OFFICER: So you broke lines to scavenge.

RANKER: To keep myself alive.

OFFICER: And you left your regimental coat behind for the same reason.

RANKER: Sir?

OFFICER: Your red coat, sir, with the gold facings, the loops and buttons and slashing that denotes the Ninth, I don't see it. Or is it under there with your stocking? Or did the rats eat it in the night? Or is that what I hear the cattle chomping on next door?

RANKER: No, sir. I left it. The white revers do rather show up against the red, even at night.

OFFICER: And they denote a soldier.

RANKER: You want to keep them smart, sir.

OFFICER: How admirable. What daring to remove yourself from a secure and guarded encampment after sundown, leaving your significant dress to preserve it and avoid detection. That's the initiative of a true English private soldier. To look for food, at night, in his shirt — in his white shirt — in November. What sort of fool do you think me, soldier?

RANKER: I don't, sir, I don't. It's the truth.

OFFICER: You have no proper uniform and no danger from the rebel sentries because they look out for you. Look out for you not as a quarry but as an accomplice.

RANKER: No, sir. I told you, I'm the King's man.

OFFICER: You work for them, soldier . What's your name?

RANKER: Smith.

    [THE OFFICER *laughs in disbelief.*]

No it is. Ned Smith.

OFFICER: What absurdity is this?

RANKER: I can't help it, sir. A lot of people are called Smith. And I'm one of them.

OFFICER: Of course. Smith on Tuesday, Brown on Wednesday, Jones on Thursday. What did your mother call you?

RANKER: Ned.

OFFICER: Yes, to be sure. It's an irate mother that calls her son by his patronymic. What did your schoolmaster call you?

RANKER: I never had one.

OFFICER: That I believe. What do the Americans call you?

RANKER: I don't know — Lord North's spaniel, Farmer George's footslogger, Redback — I don't know. I don't talk to them and they don't talk to me.

OFFICER: My friend, somebody gives them information, not just their own scouts, not just the savages. Oh, we know some of Arnold's men and some of Gates's men turned their coats and came to us only to turn back again when they'd learned something useful and carry it off as a lapdog's bone to their fellow rebels. But there are also fellows, low despicable fellows, who have betrayed their King and their comrades-in-arms for some private gain. Such fellows take their coats right off and quite probably call themselves Smith.

RANKER: I haven't. I promise. I promise. What would be the point?

OFFICER: The point would be money, comfort, revenge, the attractions of some colonial girl; all sorts of affections can overtake the human heart.

RANKER: But the fighting's over, sir. What would the point be for the rebels? If I was a traitor, sir — and I'm not — what use could I be to them?

OFFICER: [*after a thoughtful pause*] General Burgoyne could tell you. After the battle of Bemis Heights he had not one picture card left in his hand. The generals and the armies that should have joined him at Albany had failed to do so. And he now knew that they would not do so. His own forces were depleted and exhausted, having been exposed for too long, winning battles all the way down from Canada, but losing the weather and the supplies. General Burgoyne knew this, but General Gates did not. Gates knew he had managed one defeat of an exceptional force which had operated with success and lightness of touch at Boston — well, heavy-handedly at Boston — but in the real campaign at Ticonderoga, Lake George, Skenesborough. A force which might any moment be relieved by fresh armies from New York or Philadelphia. A force to which he and all the rebels owed true allegiance as subjects of the King.

Gates hadn't seen inside the British position, didn't know what dragoons or infantry might soon threaten from the south, could only guess at the extent of the stores afloat on the Hudson, at the morale of the Hessians, Fraser's Canadians and the regiments of foot.

What Burgoyne had to do was to play on that ignorance, to shuffle, to deal, to come to the table and leave the table with a proud and jaunty step. And Burgoyne, I know, thought he carried it off.

RANKER: Well, if he couldn't, there aren't many who could.

OFFICER: He wasn't called. The cards fluttered and shifted but always face down. And Gates agreed that all the British troops should honourably withdraw, not to reappear in North America to be sure, but to march out, drums beating, flags high in the breeze. That was agreed. It wasn't victory, but it was a way short of ignominy. And achieved with a handful of apple-pips, hooded eyes and a smile.

But then, after the agreement, at the fifty-ninth minute, someone — or some two, some three — showed the rebel general what had been our general's hand. It had to be soldiers from our side, long-servers who knew the whole story not only from their orders but from inference and experience. The English were sold out, sir, two weeks ago. By men with no coats. And so the poor loyal English soldier will sit through another winter, without a respectable glass of port in sight.

RANKER: It wasn't me. I give you my word, sir.

OFFICER: What on earth can be said for a country that is prepared to make tea a political issue?

RANKER: Sir, listen to me. I am not a spy, I am not a traitor. You must believe me. I swear it on my oath to God.

OFFICER: Well, maybe. I'm not a religious man. I'm a member of the Church of England. [*Pause.*] So you're not a spy. And your name's Smith. What did your father do?

RANKER: He shoed horses.

OFFICER: That would seem to confirm the second part of your story. I'm sorry, soldier, when matters go awry suspicion takes to the high road. A defeated army, an army that knows it's defeated, feels defeated, is like a shoal of fish in a net: suffocating, ill, at war with itself, wanting only to get away.

RANKER: You don't have to tell me.

OFFICER: Why the river?

RANKER: You already answered that.

OFFICER: I did? I must pay more attention to what I say.

RANKER: When you're on the losing side all you want to do is get out of the place. You want to put it behind you, start again somewhere. The tale of my life.

OFFICER: I'm not sure I wish to understand what you're saying.

RANKER: I speak English, same as them.

OFFICER: I wouldn't go as far as that. But are you telling me, soldier, you went into the river to try and cross it? To get away on the other side? You're mad, dear boy, you'd never make it. You'd be swept away; and if the current didn't get you the cold would.

RANKER: No, I wasn't trying to swim away, sir. Private soldiers don't have maps but I've seen the Hudson in daylight — credit me with some intelligence.

OFFICER: I do, Smith, I do.

RANKER: I just wanted a change from the nothingness of being a prisoner. I took the shilling to get away from the dullness of our Surrey village. We were eight of us crammed into the attic-room over the forge. You couldn't stand up in the place. Two of my brothers died. Then my mother, giving birth to the last girl. The girl never lived either. There wasn't any work, you couldn't even take rabbits because everywhere was someone else's. So I thought, right Ned, get out. And when the chance came I took it. Marching away to the music, eight pence a day of my very own, every day, no more hunger pangs and a uniform better than all the clothes my brothers had put together, and that wouldn't be smelling of smoke.

OFFICER: But you've changed your mind?

RANKER: No. No, I haven't. It's the same thing again, that's all. There's no future in this army, is there? — with all respect, sir. We're hobbled like goats. We can't go anywhere. We can't put people in their place. I haven't been paid for four months.

OFFICER: So you took charge of your destiny.

RANKER: I don't know about that, but I don't want to live like a weevil under a stone. And no one's going to shift the stone for you.

OFFICER: Where did you think you were making for?

RANKER: Somewhere else. Like I said, I don't have any maps or charts and I couldn't read them if I had.

OFFICER: Escaping from rebel imprisonment is an honourable thing for a soldier to do, if it's to put himself back in the King's service. But running from his regiment, that's a matter for a hanging. Did you have a particular intention, Mr Smith?

RANKER: To use my wits. See if I could see what's what.

OFFICER: A dangerous course.

RANKER: I went into the river to avoid some drunken armed Colonists. If I'd been deserting I'd have joined them, wouldn't I? And I ended up in here, didn't I? By my own choice.

OFFICER: I grant you.

RANKER: And sir —
OFFICER: Yes?
RANKER: This isn't inside the stockade, either. And you also don't appear to wear a topcoat, sir.
OFFICER: Touché. I have one, and more in fact, I give my word; though I am bound to say, like you, I must live by my wits. But not from choice. And not to leave the Army, but to stay with it.
RANKER: I've told you who I am, whether or not you believe it. I think, sir, you should do the same for me. I mean, I don't know that you're an officer. You're not from the Ninth or I'd recognize you. I guess from your clothes that you're some kind of gentleman.
OFFICER: That reassures me on my choice of tailor. And 'gentleman' is a term that gratifies me, though if I've not built something more on that foundation I am simply a gallant waste of time.
RANKER: Are you a gentleman ranker? [*A thought strikes him.*] Or a gentleman plantation owner — was that what the talk of spies was about? Is that why you want to keep with the Army?
OFFICER: [*indicating the flag*] With that above my head? I have a command, Smith.
RANKER: You mean you're a colonel?
OFFICER: [*seizing it*] Yes, I am a colonel. Light Dragoons, Sixteenth, the Queen's Own.
RANKER: Not many of them here that I've seen.
OFFICER: No. I was with the Line Brigade in the last action. Twentieth, Twenty-first, Sixty-second.
RANKER: [*not picking up the significance*] Some kind of liaison then, Colonel?
OFFICER: You could say so. After supplies — ammunition, weapons, food — it's the most important thing in a war, the passing of clear and accurate orders.
RANKER: A few soldiers help as well.
OFFICER: And in the right place: you don't need to tell me that.
RANKER: So why are you in hiding, sir?
    [*The sound of voices coming nearer.*]
OFFICER: Why am I here, you mean, in this place?
    [*A shadow passes across the light. The voices are outside the window.*]
RANKER: Look out, sir, get down!

OFFICER: There's no danger.
> [THE RANKER *pulls* THE OFFICER *down, out of sight of the window.*]

RANKER: [*whispers urgently*] You don't know who they are. There are some angry men around with a mighty hatred of the likes of us. They could slit our throats in here and none would be the wiser.
> [*There is a loud knocking above, where the steps lead. Both men freeze. The knocking is repeated, followed by the sound of a door being forced back.* THE OFFICER *moves swiftly and stealthily to the other side of the room. Footsteps are heard above.*]

VOICE: [*off*] He's not here. We'll find him later.
> [*Sound of the door being pulled shut. The voices trail away. Silence.* THE OFFICER *relaxes. He gives* THE RANKER *a shrug and a quizzical smile.*]

RANKER: Sounds like they're after you, Colonel. After somebody, anyway. Be silly to get killed now, wouldn't it?

OFFICER: The Americans do seem to exhaust themselves in their determination to drive home a victory. We British have a much better system.

RANKER: We lose.

OFFICER: Yes, but we lose with style. Then we change the game. Why do you think almost every game in the known world was invented by an Englishman? Because that way we're the only people to understand the rules. It allows us to win without breaking into a sweat. The moment the others catch up — new rules! new rules! Believe me, the British dominions overseas were won and lost on the playing fields of Eton. And remember, you heard that from me first!

RANKER: Yes, sir.

OFFICER: One of the troubles with wit. It bears no identity mark. Once uttered it's anybody's with a notebook or half a brain. And there are few things so depressing, Smith, as a sally you originated being delivered back to you at a later date by some limping party who mistakes the rhythm, but claims it as his own. And is toasted for it. I'd toast him, too. At the end of a fork. You know, Smith, that I write?

RANKER: Being as you're a colonel I thought you'd probably got beyond a thumb-print.

OFFICER: Remind me to strangle you when you find your other stocking.

RANKER: My father used to throw horse-shoes.

OFFICER: Clearly a man of exquisite taste. I hope he lives long and grows rich. May we all. As I say, for amusement and occasional gain I write, I pen the odd theatre piece. I have written professional papers, too, as a soldier. But there are few wounds worse than to be attacked in the broadsheets for the paucity of a line which the miserable scribbler then misquotes. Horace Walpole did that to me — deliberately — because I foiled the promotion of a cousin of his so corrupt that a Surbiton brothel-keeper would have shone white beside him. Not, of course, that I've ever been to Surbiton. Far too much low life. And a little too far from London.

RANKER: You write plays?

OFFICER: Oh yes. Well, a couple. And I have an idea for another.

RANKER: You didn't write the one in Boston?

OFFICER: "The Blockade of Boston"? Yes.

RANKER: After Bunker Hill?

OFFICER: Yes.

RANKER: Oh my God. I know who you are. You're not a colonel. Oh . . . My . . . God!

OFFICER: No, that would be an overstatement.
    [THE RANKER *stands to rigid attention.*]
Please be easy.

RANKER: You're . . . you're him.

OFFICER: I'm your General Officer Commanding, yes.

RANKER: Gentleman Johnny.

OFFICER: The title I like best.

RANKER: Gentleman Johnny Burgoyne.

OFFICER: Your servant, sir.

RANKER: It's not fair. You're not wearing your general's . . . . I mean it's not fair, I've never seen you without your wig before so how could I know? And anyway, sir, you lied: you said you were a colonel when I asked.

OFFICER: I don't think I lied, Smith. I just gave short weight with the truth. For I am a colonel, as I said, Colonel of the Queen's Regiment of Dragoons, and proud of it. The first regiment of mounted soldiers in the British Army who are capable of swift offensive action. Indeed, of any action at all, since the British tradition has always been to arm the cavalry so heavily that the least counterblow in an engagement meant they fell off, usually sinking out of sight under the weight of their own defences. This was thought good by successive War Ministers as it preserved them intact to fight another day and therefore saved the taxpayers money. Since, when that other day dawned, all they would do is roll sideways to disappear in some fresh peat-bog, it's hard to divine where the advantage of having them lay. Their main contribution was to afford target practice for the enemy. An unusual aim for government policy.

However, a quarter of a century ago I was on the continent of Europe, in a private capacity, and took the opportunity to observe the competition.

From this it occurred to me that we should do well if our dragoons were horsemen rather than equine cargo, and that they should have a knowledge of tack and tactics, be credited with initiative and enthusiasm; after all, the Englishman's saving virtue has always been that he's the most bloody-minded animal this side of a camel. I favoured using this. The Prussians prefer terrorising their men into mindless submission, the French used to employ an honour system entirely; as a result of which they were charming and utterly unreliable. It gave *us* high hopes of reclaiming Calais. In the light of this and their disasters in the Seven Years War, their officers moved to Prussian methods and most of their men moved elsewhere.

RANKER: They've got a way of setting things up, though, the French, haven't they?

OFFICER: They're brilliant strategists. The best contemporary works on warfare are by the French. But they falter at carrying it through.

RANKER: They've a lot of style, though, sir.

OFFICER: Well, everyone says it's their supreme quality, but I don't believe it. It's the English who truly love style. Tell an Englishman what to do, order him to do it, and he'll do the reverse. That's style. Leave him to his own devices and he would die rather than admit embarrassment, be poisoned in preference to being seen objecting to the food, walk a mile with a nail in his boot rather than interrupt the conversation. And that's style, too. By comparison the French are shrewd but clumsy. I've always thought that when Hobbes described life as nasty, brutish and short, he had the French in mind.

RANKER: Be fair, sir, the English can be pretty rough too.

OFFICER: Well, maybe. But that's one of those no-way-out complaints, isn't it? If you describe someone as ugly or fair, or as mean or generous, it's clear which condition is thought to be desirable. But when you say the English are rough I'd hardly be defending them by saying no, they're not, they're very smooth. Even their best friends describe them as slippery. Not much of a compliment is it? Outside the upper echelons of the Tory Party.

RANKER: What I mean is I don't think we're that different from everybody else. We can all be smart; we can all be vicious.

OFFICER: You are Lord North's spaniel, aren't you? You don't let go — that's English bloody-mindedness all right. Don't worry my boy, I like you for it. Of course faults and merits are common to all humanity; some preponderate in one group, some in another. But I might ask you whether you've witnessed a flogging during these campaigns?

RANKER: No, well, it's hardly ever allowed now, is it?

OFFICER: Not in my army, no, but I've always preferred beating the enemy to beating my own soldiers. You won't have been sworn at, either.

RANKER: I wouldn't be sure of that, sir.

OFFICER: You shouldn't have been. It's forbidden under the Code of Military Conduct I drew up quite a while ago.

RANKER: Some of the NCOs don't seem to worry about that. Nor do some of the Americans.

OFFICER: Then the NCOs are answerable. Not the Americans of course. But then they are only Englishmen who couldn't make it at home.

RANKER: They made it last month, though, didn't they?

OFFICER: Yes, dammit, they did.

RANKER: This was a good army. You're right. I've served under a few before.

OFFICER: Who?

RANKER: Here? General Gage, then General Clinton for just a short time. This was the best lot. I mean, it was tough.

OFFICER: I know that.

RANKER: Shifting those felled trees. But we knew where we were heading, what the point of it was. Except at the end when it came apart. I felt I mattered. Me. Like at Wood Creek when that girl was scalped and the savage who did it wasn't executed — you explained why. No one had ever bothered to tell us why before.

OFFICER: When the defeat and the victories are all ancient history, I'd like to think that the ordinary soldiers, my soldiers, will speak of "the Burgoyne touch," and speak of it affectionately.

RANKER: What went wrong, sir?

OFFICER: Oh, that's a big subject.

RANKER: It's just I'd like to know why we're prisoners.

> [THE OFFICER *looks at him.*]

OFFICER: Because the battle went wrong. The battle went wrong because the campaign went wrong. If the campaign went wrong you should look to see if the plan was right. And whether or not the plan was right one thing is certain: in the first place government policy went wrong. Otherwise there need have been no war, no plan, no campaign, no battle.

RANKER: And no work for soldiers.

OFFICER: Oh, there'd be that. The first job of a soldier is to defend. To be there, no more. That's why we put him in such a vivid uniform — so that no one can mistake his presence.

RANKER: I thought the red coat was so the blood wouldn't show.

OFFICER: No. The Prussians wear blue, the French wear green — it's to impress. And the Americans . . . . come as they are. The first mistake was to unite New York and New Hampshire, Connecticut and Pennsylvania against His Majesty's government. They'd always been perfectly happy before, sniping at each other. Much like Queen Anne and the Duchess of Marlborough.

RANKER: When was that?

OFFICER: Before you were born. The reason for this unity, as I'm sure you know, was because permission was given to the East India Company to export tea to America. This would have halved its price in the Colonies and taken the trade out of the hands of the smugglers who had it. The English, after all, are a moral people who profoundly object to any abuse when control of it falls into *other* people's hands. It doesn't matter whether it's smuggling or bribe-taking or cozenage. Other people must not do it! And for reasons I cannot understand the Americans weren't grateful for this. Except I can understand. I spoke out against it in the Commons.

RANKER: It was the taxation thing, wasn't it?

OFFICER: That was a nonsense. "No taxation without representation". Every one of the Colonies here has its own legislating assembly — tell that to Lancashire — and the cost of all these parliaments is borne by the squires of England. Do you realize I pay twenty-five shillings a year tax?

RANKER: That's about what I have to spend in a year.

OFFICER: And do you know what the average Colonist pays? Sixpence. That'll change now. They'll discover the cost of defence. No, the reason I spoke out against it in the Commons was not that the duty should be abolished, but that persuasion is a better victor than force. Of course the Americans don't see it our way — I'm a playwright, I'm practised at seeing not only my view but the other man's too — they are here, this side of the ocean, because they disliked what they were born to in England, as in some sense you are, too. Treat the other man with respect, listen to him, talk to him. And in time you'll find agreement. The politics of agreement is the only politics worth following. And for the most practical of reasons: it's the only one that lasts.

Governments, unfortunately, seem slow to appreciate this. They think it's weak and they like to be thought strong.

RANKER: Well, it's no good lying down in front of the enemy, is it? You've got to let them know what's what.

OFFICER: But so often it's letting them know what's what that turns them into the enemy. I have never taken the view that our argument with the Canadians and the New Englanders is irreconcilable. I have to confess that I spent the early weeks of my marriage, and happy times since, in the land of our traditional foes, the French — and my friend and host was Choiseul, now France's greatest minister. I was most generously treated. Admittedly, one had to get used to them eating horses, but once you've seen the way they ride you understand why.

RANKER: No, but when I was a boy I used to have to go to the market, six and a half miles over the hill to Farnham.

We didn't have a horse. My father shoed horses and covered wheels and made stirrups but if we had to go anywhere we walked. I was the eldest, so on Tuesdays and Fridays I had to go off at first light, keeping as warm as I could and as dry as I could, which wasn't always easy, with a sack of things to sell. When Mother was alive she used to make bonnets and I'd bring back linen and bits of ribbon for her. Cherry colour was her favourite. And there'd be trivets, and iron nails and things my father had crafted in spare moments. And sometimes things people in the village had given him in exchange for new hinges or a lock plate or repairing their shafts. And the sack was heavy — I'm talking about when I was a boy, hardly more than half the height I am now. But however heavy that sack was I carried a big poker in my other hand. Because whether I was going in the morning, or coming back at the end of the day with a coin or two in my pocket and maybe some salt or some walnuts, there were always lads waiting by the ponds up near Frensham. They were big and they were several. With the poker in my hand they kept their distance.

OFFICER: But that's the musket, fife and drum. The deliberate show. The warning. It's not the same as cracking their skulls.

RANKER: If they'd come near me I'd have cracked their skulls and they knew it. If I'd stopped to talk I'd have ended in the pond and our victuals and money would have gone off in their pockets. That's the only agreement that would have been reached.

OFFICER: I don't doubt that is an astute assessment. Would I be right in hazarding that while this overcame the problem it avoided the actual use of force?

RANKER: Except once. Tobias Crutchley got his arm broke when he grabbed my scarf.

OFFICER: Was there retribution later?

RANKER: Of course not. He was twelve. Old enough to hang.

OFFICER: I see. Then it was the greater threat that stopped him rather than your lesser action.

RANKER: Not really.

OFFICER: How so?

RANKER: He went on robbing. When he was seventeen or thereabouts he took himself to London to avoid the magistrates. A gentleman shot him dead on Cambridge Heath.

OFFICER: During a robbery?

RANKER: Crutchley fired first. He packed his pistol with powder but had forgotten to put a ball in. I laughed myself drunk when I heard.

OFFICER: Sounds something like the order of things in this campaign. With a not dissimilar result.

RANKER: We're still alive, sir.

OFFICER: And I hope you will be for many years, Smith. My own future is less certain.

RANKER: What do you mean, sir? They don't shoot generals.

OFFICER: They took aim at an admiral not so long ago. And they didn't miss. Which is not at all encouraging. And he only lost an island. I'll be blamed for a continent. However, we're counselled to live every day as though it is our last.

RANKER: My mother used to say, live as though it's your first.

OFFICER: The same thing, better expressed.

RANKER: The other officers will speak for you, sir.

OFFICER: They won't be given the chance. I only hope I will be. That, my good soldier, is why I am down here. I am sequestered in this building, with my lodging above, naturally. The cattle belong to some Colonist with a finger missing who started life in Buckinghamshire. I came down here to order my thoughts. To plan how I shall conduct myself at my impeachment or court martial, or whatever lies in store.

RANKER: Can they do that?

OFFICER: I hope they will! The alternative will be condemnation. Humiliation without right of reply. I need a court to be exonerated. [*Pause.*] You asked what went wrong.

RANKER: I meant in last month's battle.

OFFICER: Can't be understood that way. The fruit of the vine is determined by the soil it's rooted in.

RANKER: And walnuts and cherries and pippins.

[THE OFFICER *looks straight at him, then smiles.*]

OFFICER: I'd forgotten you're a Surrey countryman. What went wrong at Bemis Heights last month had gone wrong much, much earlier. You said you served under my schoolfellow, General Gage. Well, when the Prime Minister, Lord North, advised me that the King had told me off for America, it was as Howe's deputy in New

York. The general in Canada was to be Clinton. Gage of course was Commander-in-Chief.

As my interest in organization and strategy was known, and was not shared by all officers of field rank — some prefer Vauxhall Pleasure Gardens — I was ordered to devise a campaign strategy to reduce the rebellion. My own role, of course, would be subsidiary, but it was thought I might energize others. I remember Governor Hutchinson of Massachusetts complaining of the want of vigorous direction as we sat one morning taking a syllabub. It was a not uncommon view.

And the strategy, loosely, was this.

Boston — as you know, you were there — was the hub for discontent. It would have to be evacuated. And so it was in the kind of victory that makes defeat look attractive. I had advised the King's ministers that no army sent from England would be equal to the task of subduing all the colonies on its own. We would need the support of the Southern blacks whom we should arm, of the Indians whose intelligence and scouting would be vital, and possibly decisive if turned against us. We should need well-trained foreign troops, and we would be wise morally as well as tactically to raise levies among those Colonists loyal to the Crown, to support each of two main armies: one based in New York to subdue New England; one in Governor Carleton's Canada to achieve the same pacification there.

The two armies should thrust towards each other through the fighting months and conjoin at Albany in the north of this state of New York, before the onset of winter. Supplies to the Canadian army would then be assured through the New England seaports.

The government in England approved this policy and adopted it while reducing the number of men made available in every theatre of activity, thus pleasing the voters and endangering the expedition. But it is the mark of the politician everywhere to seek advice from those who should know and then to claim to know better.

I would gladly remind them of this on my return. Which is not to attack Lord North. I have a great deal of time for Lord North. Which is well, as he thinks very slowly. It took him some months to perceive that General

Gage, an officer of many parts, nonetheless had one or two missing.

RANKER: He should have seen him from where I was standing.

OFFICER: Gage didn't always get the support he deserved either, though I think he was better served than I.

RANKER: Sir, he never did anything. He sat there and watched the rebel numbers grow. He had less energy than grass.

OFFICER: Well, well.

RANKER: That can't be right, can it? You have to strike. Keep the advantage.

OFFICER: In my book, too, Smith; and after a while the King's Ministers agreed. General Gage was asked home.

RANKER: I remember the day he went.

OFFICER: General Howe took his place. And I was given command of the Northern Army. Not something I had expected.

RANKER: I remember when you talked to the whole army, too, soon after you'd taken over. Couldn't hear all of it.

OFFICER: It was windier than I would have liked.

RANKER: Oh no, I don't think it was too long. It was just I couldn't hear because I was at the back.

OFFICER: I didn't mean that. Although there were plenty in England who thought what I said was florid and dull. Quite a few compared it unfavourably with General Wolfe's address to *his* army, before they attacked the French. Very harsh. Since in most particulars my address *was* General Wolfe's. I'd long admired it as exemplary so I stole most of it on the principle that the sincerest form of flattery is theft.

Then, as you know, we faced the realities of an army fighting on a continent not its own. By which I don't mean to suggest we lacked a right in being here. The Colonists had always had our protection; it was quite proper that we should have their allegiance. But when you are not familiar with the terrain, when today's friendly face may be tomorrow's assassin, or even tonight's, and when the government you answer to is months away by message, then matters are harder than they might be.

RANKER: The cold was the worst. Made me think fondly of dark snowy days in Frensham. One thing about the forge — it was always warm.

OFFICER: I'm afraid there's another winter here for most of us.

If the Convention I concluded with the Americans had not been broken by them you might have been home for Christmas. Not now, I fear.

RANKER: I'm not afraid, sir. I was only truly afraid once in this campaign. I don't mean the tang in your mouth and the tenseness in your legs that tells you you could jump ten feet in the air, straight up, if you determine. You get that in any battle. You get it when you hear the Indians give their cry. Sometimes when the Sergeant-Major strides towards you gripped by his spleen.

OFFICER: That's the apprehension that concentrates the mind.

RANKER: Right, sir. But when we had the first battle here, sir, we were in the reserve.

OFFICER: With the Ninth, yes.

RANKER: We were called forward in the afternoon. I was alongside Hugo Syrett — just another soldier, sir, like me. He was a year or two older but we joined the same time. We messed together, saw to each other's strapping if we were in full regimentals. If my powder was damp he'd give me some of his. He could be ill-tempered, morose more, when the sun came up after a night together in an ale-house. But once he'd puked and freshened his breath with spruce beer he was companionable again. That was it with Hugo. He was there, always himself. Knew him like a glove. Always blushed if you mentioned Piltdown Pam.

We stood shoulder to shoulder, like we did for most fusillades, another lot kneeling in front of us. Sometimes I'd catch him with my elbow as we tried to reload fast and he'd growl an oath from the side of his mouth. "You got a bite like a whore's muff" was his favourite. Then I'd know we were all right. Only suddenly, that day back in September, I had all the elbow-room in the world. I looked down. Hugo was on his back. And his face, his solid old face, was in little bits. Looked like a china cup smashed on a plate of offal. I couldn't hear the muskets any more, just gulls squawking.

[*A long pause.*]

No one to talk to now. No one who's been to Guildford mop.

OFFICER: Another Surrey man?

RANKER: Sussex. But he'd travelled. [*Pause.*] Then we advanced.

Had to leave him behind. All the side of his face in bits. I don't know what happened after that. I just know it all went wrong from then.

OFFICER: There's nothing I can say, soldier. The loss of a comrade, the loss of a loved one, is a loss of part of oneself. And Time as the great healer? That's the great lie. It heals nothing. Merely, in time, one remembers less often. The spirit tires of the pain. When you remember your friend Syrett I'm sure it touches you as hard as the moment you saw him fall. I know. There are names in my heart, too.

>[*Pause.*]

RANKER: If we'd won the war I could have made more sense of it. There'd seem to be some point. He was dead for nothing.

OFFICER: I know. I know.

RANKER: He hadn't been paid for four months either.

OFFICER: None of us. Was he married?

RANKER: Yes.

OFFICER: Then you can do something for him. See that the pay he is due reaches his widow.

>[*Short pause.*]

RANKER: Why didn't we go on winning?

OFFICER: In practical terms?

RANKER: Well, you only ever see the bit of fighting you're involved with. And at Saratoga we didn't know what was happening — we were back in reserve for the first few hours.

OFFICER: You remember we were camped around Sword's house, close to the river? We had to be close to the river — it was the one way to transport the great weight of supplies an army in alien territory must provide itself with. At nine in the morning we began the first stage of an advance on three fronts. General Fraser's column, very mixed, Canadians and Indians and Loyalists, and because they were the vanguard, the best marksmen from any regiment under my command. They marched out due west towards Saratoga Lake, to secure our right flank.

RANKER: Sorry sir, don't follow.

OFFICER: Look. This is Sword's house —

>[*He indicates his 'desk'.*]

>The river.

[*He lays a scarf on the floor, upstage/downstage, left of his 'desk'.*]

You are Saratoga Lake.

[*He moves* THE RANKER *some way stage right, roughly in line with the 'desk' and clear of the area where the troop movements will be shown.*]

Fraser's column marched 2½ miles this way then swung south towards the farm, Freeman's farm, which marked the rebels' furthest line of advance, coming as they did from *here* . . .

[*He goes as far as he can downstage centre and puts his back to the audience, demonstrating for them that their view of the battle is exactly that of the Americans.*]

At ten in the morning, just as Fraser's advanced corps were wheeling into the sun, the rest of the Army, still here, began to move. General Riedesel and his Brunswickers and Hessians, with General Phillips' heavy artillery which I was retaining for later or if necessary, defensive use, proceeded alongside the river. The Germans first in a long phalanx; General Phillips, whose guns could move only slowly, here behind.

At the same time, the great boats on the Hudson, comprising extra stores and ammunition, and the surgeon's needs, weighed anchor and made upstream. Ahead of them, guard boats under the command of the 47th. The guard boats instructed, naturally, to assure the safety of the bateaux that lay astern, but also to proceed a short way behind the Germans whose task was to secure the adjacent land.

At the exact moment that General Riedesel and the ships set forth, the centre column raised its colours and marched along the same track as Fraser's men had used. This, as you know, was the British brigade. After a mile and a half we too turned to face the sun. The three land prongs and the one water-borne moved steadily on the American position, entrenched on Bemis Heights.

Given the territory — woods, ravines, broken bridges — our progress was fair. I and my fellow generals had personally reconnoitred on horseback a day or two before, so we knew what to expect. I commanded from the middle of the British brigade. That made me most available to everyone and put me in the best position to judge the progress of the battle. Orderly subalterns kept me in continual communication with all officers in command, the subalterns reporting to and from the left flank being French-speakers.

RANKER: Was that to trick the Americans?

OFFICER: No, the reason was that Riedesel has good English but most of his colonels do not. However, all of them speak French. So had Riedesel fallen, with the messages in French none would have been lost or misunderstood.

RANKER: But the messages to General Fraser were still in English?

OFFICER: Indeed they were and as we trudged towards the rebels, pockets of General Fraser's troops peeled off to protect the right flank and the rear. A unit here, a unit there and there.

      [He indicates.]

RANKER: Was that likely to be the first place they'd attack then, sir?

OFFICER: Yes, we thought that was the greatest danger. You see the river protected us like a moat, but it also hemmed us in. On this flank we could be turned and forced back. Then the river would prove a prison wall; and a graveyard. To reduce this danger General Phillips towed a bridge his men had engineered behind one of the bateaux. This would give access to the far side of the Hudson, an escape funnel if we needed it.

The Americans outnumbered us by more than two to one. Nonetheless it was not until 12.45 — lunchtime — that we were involved in any serious skirmishing. We were this side of a valley, two of the three columns having swung to their right to present a solid front. Ahead of us, on higher ground on the other side, lay Freeman's farm. I deputed a small number of our men to clear it.

RANKER: There were twenty or more of us from the Ninth.

OFFICER: Indeed. And the same from other battalions.

RANKER: Under our Major Forbes.

OFFICER: Was that the action where your friend was killed?

RANKER: It was later in the afternoon. Once we started firing, the small group of us I mean, we found there were quite a few troops in that house.

OFFICER: You're right. And our action seemed to wake the Americans on the heights behind. General Arnold's troops launched themselves briefly at General Fraser's, whom they seemed surprised to find. I called up some of our cannon from the rear and when they had put two large holes through the main building of the farm the rebels remembered more pressing engagements and left. Unfortunately but unsurprisingly they left only to re-group and attack our centre. My flanking generals could not support the centre with too many of their own men as we had no knowledge whether General Gates might not release the main body of his army from the heights and prise apart any weakened area of our front. So we contended with General Arnold's onslaughts as we were. And we withstood.

RANKER: Hugo didn't.

OFFICER: The cost was high. And the profit was little except in honour. But this was less than half the plan. The plan was for a conjunction south of where we are. Daily I expected General Clinton to arrive with an army down the Hudson. Daily I expected General Howe, who for reasons of his own had taken his army into Pennsylvania to swing north and join the fray from here.

[*He indicates downstage right.*]

Then, like the claws of a crab, we would have the Americans encircled. I expected them because it was in the plan, and they were already overdue. There was no question of the plan's requirements, no question of its interpretation. I had written it. Germain and North had approved it. The King had ordered it. It was no longer *my* plan. It was the King's order. I sent ten separate messengers to General Howe. General Howe! General When, more like. Not one came to me in reply. Anyway, we held our line, at a cost of your friend Hugo and some three hundred more killed and wounded. And the dark descended on the first day of battle.

[*Brief pause.*]

Next morning I proposed to sharpen our attack and prise the rebels from their hill. But Simon Fraser persuaded me the men were too fatigued. He was undoubtedly right.

RANKER: I think he was, sir.

OFFICER: So I held the attack, which would be our break towards

Albany, until the next day. Which, with the earth steaming through a coat of frost, brought news at last from the south. Clinton was on his way, pushing up through Montgomery. All we had to do was hold. I sent messengers every night to General Clinton from then on. Hourly expecting him to push Gates from his perch and . . .

[*He pulls a blanket from the bed to demonstrate.*]

. . . Howe to smother what remained of Arnold's men as they and the others made off across the Hudson by the bridge which we could see they had hastily built. What I could not know then was that Howe had left Clinton with hardly any men to spare.

What I could not know was that the ministers in London had left General Howe without news that the plan, with which he was familiar, which we had all discussed, had been adopted as the Government's policy. So we sat, and froze and bled, confident. We had no stomach to retreat. As week succeeded day, I received no orders to retreat. Not from Clinton. Not from Howe. We dug in, losing a few more men each day in this exchange or that. Then my lines of communication back to Canada came under attack. I was powerless to defend them. Next, fresh rebels came at us from the east. After a month we were beleaguered. As you know, I pulled us back to Saratoga . . .

[*He goes upstage centre to the foot of the ladder.*]

. . . to reform our defences. We had three days food, well less, but we had been on half-rations for so long that it would have lasted us three days, and we were by now outnumbered four to one.

So I sent a major to talk terms. Then like a good gamester I rejected them. And General Gates, worried by rumours of Clinton's advance, accepted the terms I offered. He didn't know, as I then did, the feebleness of Clinton's force. And in truth the terms I offered were no more than an insouciant gesture from the gallows. That's how it is, my young friend, that we stopped winning.

RANKER: They can't blame *you*.

OFFICER: There's no one else. I must account to the King's ministers. It was their failure to inform Howe, and Howe's failure to act on what he already knew, that brought about this pass. I think they won't find against themselves. Nor against General Howe. His brother is the Minister for War. Much simpler to find against me: my plan; my surrender.

RANKER: It's not right. We all know different.

OFFICER: You know because you have heard more than most. I'll thank you not to take advantage of that.

RANKER: I give you my word. But I don't just mean knowing we were let down. That was obvious to all of us, sir, though of course no one told us about the other generals. We know different because we took part in the battles before. A soldier knows when he's well-drilled and well-prepared and he likes it. Because that way he's got the best chance to win quickly and to live. And even in England they must know about what you did in Portugal before.

OFFICER: You're too young to remember that.

RANKER: No, I wasn't there. Some of the older soldiers were, and some of the sergeants. And they talked about it. Said it was a quick change of plan by you at the last moment saved the day.

OFFICER: That's right.

RANKER: And hardly anyone got killed. Valencia — that the place?

OFFICER: Valencia.

RANKER: There you are. The government must know that.

OFFICER: A politician's memory seldom goes further than his own last promotion.

RANKER: Well, forget 'em, sir. Do the other things you do.

OFFICER: Hm?

RANKER: Your plays and pamphlets.

OFFICER: I shall take up my pen only to defend my generalship and my career. General Wolfe said he would rather have written Gray's 'Elegy' than take Quebec. Having seen Quebec, I sympathize. But if you ask me whether I would prefer to have a play of mine succeed at Drury Lane or to have won at Saratoga, I must tell you I have enjoyed the pleasure of the first and I would sacrifice it a hundred times to be victorious for my country. I am a general first, a professional soldier all my life; a politician second; and a scribbler only because a gentleman ought to have a hobby for when the ladies are absent. It's cheaper than card-playing.

RANKER: The Boston play was good, though. I hadn't seen a play before, not in a room, like. The best bit was that great bombardment of guns at the beginning. I liked that.

OFFICER: That wasn't part of the play. They were real. The rebels were blowing the roofs off the town. Admittedly with a fine sense of timing. But if you like convincing noises off you should go to see a play at the Haymarket when we are returned. They have the finest thunder in London.

RANKER: I don't know that a soldier's pay would run to that, even when he gets it.

OFFICER: It's only a penny in the gods so long as you forgo an orange. And if you have the chance, see Mrs Barry, a slender woman and a luminous performer. Her husband is an Irish actor of some spirit, Mr Spranger Barry. Spranger. How he came by that name I have no idea. I like to think some querulous vicar dropped him at his baptism and the name just slipped out.

RANKER: Has Mrs Barry been in one of your plays?

OFFICER: No, no. Mrs Abingdon has, which was quite a catch.

RANKER: What about Mrs Burgoyne, sir, is she an actress?

OFFICER: My wife is dead.

RANKER: I'm sorry, sir.

OFFICER: She became ill three years ago. She died while we have been out here. March last year.

RANKER: Sorry.

OFFICER: And she wasn't an actress, no. Her parents were the Earl and Countess of Derby.

RANKER: Oh, I didn't mean no insult.

OFFICER: My dear boy, don't worry. Her parents thought my offer of marriage an insult when we were young. I was an acceptable decoration for the drawing room but an unsuitable suitor for their daughter's hand. My father being in prison at the time may have coloured their view.

RANKER: They wouldn't have liked that even in Frensham.

OFFICER: Quite.

RANKER: What did he do?

OFFICER: He played cards with a courage that outran his finances. And I was clearly his son, for I was paying court in exactly the same style. Though I came off rather better.

RANKER: You got her with child, did you?

OFFICER: No, Smith, I did not! Well, not until later. We eloped.

I ran away with her. The Earl was a good old stick, and when we came back he and Lady Derby forgave us. They stood by me throughout my adult life. They died, both of them, just before my wife. I've lost so much recently, people may well mistake me for King John. Do you have a wife, Smith?

RANKER: On my pay?

OFFICER: No good waiting till you can afford one. The land would never be peopled.

RANKER: That's the bit I look forward to. A bit of peopling. But Hugo told some frightening stories about a girl he used to do it with.

OFFICER: Piltdown Pam?

RANKER: That's incredible! You knew her too! She must have been with everybody!

OFFICER: I haven't been with her, Smith! You mentioned her earlier. It's not a name one readily forgets.

RANKER: Made a lot of people ill, she did.

OFFICER: That's why you should marry. Find a lass you really love. And between you encompass the world. Saves going out for meals too. My word, am I looking forward to a proper English dinner: a river trout, a partridge or two, some roast beef, roast lamb, a couple of slices of venison, topped off with raspberries and washed down with a bottle or two of claret. All they seem to live on here is maize and sour milk. It's no wonder they spend so much time praying.

RANKER: That would feed me for a month.

OFFICER: Pish! I've seen soldiers eat.

RANKER: I'm with you about home, though. There's nowhere like England.

OFFICER: It's sometimes said God especially favours the English. That's why He gave us a beautiful island on the edge of a continent and on the edge of an ocean. Quite why he gave us the Scots as well I don't know.

RANKER: No one else would have 'em, sir.

OFFICER: Never underestimate the intelligence of the ordinary English soldier.

RANKER: Will it be hard, being at home without your wife, sir?

OFFICER: Insupportable.

RANKER: My father was never the same after Mum died. He shrank. He still did the same things, worked the bellows, hammered out the metal, still talked friendly to people. But he seemed smaller, greyer. Didn't shout when he was angry.

> [THE OFFICER *sits on the bed and lowers his head.*]

OFFICER: He didn't want to break the silence. That way he could still see her, hear her. He was listening just as you said you listened to the gulls, screaming. Charlotte was an extraordinary woman. I'm sure your mother was, too.

> [*He goes to get up and puts his hand on the filled missing stocking, He looks at it.*]

What on earth's this?

> [*He lifts it.*]

You seem to have a spare leg.

RANKER: That's my missing stocking.

OFFICER: Yes, but it's not unoccupied. Either the bugs are getting bigger or . . .

> [*He starts emptying it onto the bed.*]

. . . you have been indulging in an age-old military offence.

RANKER: Just a few things I wanted to keep safe.

OFFICER: From their owners.

RANKER: They won't be using them any more.

OFFICER: Some cloth, a snuff box, shoe buckles, a clock — an American clock.

> [*He looks at* THE RANKER.]

What possible use can that have? As soon as you're back in England it'll be five hours slow.

RANKER: [*truly worried*] Sir.

OFFICER: Well, at least there are no scalps. And you don't appear to have taken the Falkland Islands either. Do you remember that? Seven years ago? No, far too young. Some hotheads from Buenos Aires invaded the Falklands. Heaven knows what for. And Old Pitt wanted to fight a war over it. He'd reached his dotage. The Commons voted to send a ship down to guard them and that did the trick. So long as no one is idiotic enough to withdraw the ship there'll be no more trouble, I'll be bound. As I said before, defence needs to be visible. Then it works. Well, most of the time, anyway. Keep your baubles, boy. But don't take any more.

RANKER: Thank you, sir.

OFFICER: Do I hear footsteps?

> [*Sound of same.*]

RANKER: Oh God, they're back.

> [*Loud knocking on the door above.* THE OFFICER *gestures for a confident stillness. The knocking is repeated.*]

OFFICER: Let's prepare to meet whoever it is. Look your smartest. Here, wear this.

> [*He throws* THE RANKER *an embroidered sash.* THE RANKER *pulls on his stocking and boots. A third brief knocking and then the sound of the door above being opened.*]

Tie this round your waist.

> [*He gives* THE RANKER *the scarf that was the Hudson river.*]

VOICE: [*off*] General Burgoyne! General Burgoyne!

OFFICER: Your servant, sir. I'll wait upon you in a moment. [*to* THE RANKER, *inspecting him and putting his dress right*] That's good. That's smart. Now let's go up and see what the world has to say.

RANKER: [*at the bottom of the ladder*] After you, sir.

OFFICER: What?

RANKER: After you, sir. Etiquette.

OFFICER: Etiquette! Etiquette says tip your plate away from you so if it falls the porage goes all over your friend opposite. I'll stick with good manners and good sense.

RANKER: Then after you, sir, as good manners.

OFFICER: Yes, but good sense says that if I go first you'll clear the room of my possessions. I'll keep you where I can see you, Smith. After you!

VOICE: [*off*] General Burgoyne! Sorry to press you, sir, I'm a little late for a christening. But I'd like to present my compliments. The Reverend Richard Dudgeon: I do hope you remember me.

OFFICER: Oh, I remember you, sir, I remember you. Mr Smith, march on.

RANKER: How do you march up a ladder?

OFFICER: Easy. Imagine the rungs are cabinet ministers' heads. That's the way!

> [THE RANKER *exits up the ladder.*]

Not that they're *quite* thick enough.

> [THE OFFICER *looks around.*]

It was a great plan. Was it not, Charlotte? A great plan.

> [*He starts to ascend.*]

Your servant, Mr Dudgeon!

> [*Then the light swiftly fades.*]

THE END

My Sister Next Door

CHARACTERS

ANTHEA

GWEN

ANTHEA and GWEN are sisters in their middle age, Gwen being a few years older than Anthea. Both roles may be played by the same actress.

The play is in two acts, each set in separate but adjacent rooms in what was once the family house in the respectable village of Duffield not far from Derby.

The time is the present.

Each act lasts thirty-five minutes and an interval is required between them.

My Sister Next Door was first performed at the Prairie Theatre Exchange, Winnipeg on 15th July 1989, followed by a Canadian tour. It was directed by Michael Burrell with the following cast:

ANTHEA:

GWEN: } .... Anna Barry

Sponsored by the British Council

The play was first presented in London at the Latchmere Theatre, Battersea on 14th May 1990, with the same cast and director.

FOREWORD

The one-person play is an opportunity to focus on a single life and to go some way towards realizing that old Jewish saying that a single life represents the whole world.

It presents a number of technical problems: for the performer it requires not only energy but a startling degree of concentration; for the writer finding the variety of tone and pace, varying the emotional pitch within a single speech so that it continually engages and surprises the audience, is an absorbing exercise.

Interestingly, solo plays have become more popular in recent years. Partly because they are economic to produce and transport at a time when investment in the arts is thought to be a handout while investment in commerce is thought to be a duty, even a privilege for the investor. Nonetheless, audiences who a generation ago would only turn out to see a lone actor if he were a big star re-hashing highlights of his career, or highlights of somebody else's, are more adventurous and sometimes well rewarded for it: *Judgment,* the Fo/Rame plays for a woman alone, *Shirley Valentine* are fine pieces of work by any standard.

Having been fairly early in the field with the full-length play *Hess* (1978) I thought that with *My Sister Next Door* I would try to get the best of two worlds. Not merely to present a pair of sisters who share some characteristics, some quirks of vocabulary and experience, yet in essential ways contrast with each other, but also to put each in a perspective through the eyes of the other. So at the end of the first half you think you know Anthea and have some idea of what her sister will be like. At the end of the second act you realize how different Gwen is from your expectations and can understand why Anthea saw her as she did. And without having seen Anthea again your view of her, too, has measurably altered. At least, I hope so. The fun for me was in creating tension and drama between two people who never meet in the play's span and to keep the audience's perception of them shifting. In a solo piece I think that is the vital ingredient for it to work.

Since, a while ago, I worked in Derby over an extended period and stayed in Duffield, both places I like, I had better make it clear that neither the women nor the institutions they invest their lives in are modelled on particular examples. Details are authentic but borrowed from all over.

Michael Burrell
Norfolk: January 1990

Anna Barry as Anthea. Photograph courtesy of the *Edmonton Journal*.

ACT ONE

Anthea

ANTHEA *is a sunny sort of woman, very oddly attired. She has a slight Derbyshire accent. Her room is a mess.*

She comes partially into view.

Bye! . . . Bye. Next week. All right, see you then. Don't do anything I couldn't do. Bye, love. What? Oh, you're wicked! Bye.
    [*She comes in fully.*]
He's a card. Known him for years. So's his wife.

Now, what have I got time for? Oh God, look at that! It's just as well I never joined the Guides, I'd not have survived, d'ye know? I'd've been on Barn Owl's naughty girls' parade every other day. Still, you've got to accept what you are, haven't you? And make the best of it. I'm just born mucky. No, I mean, if I drop a piece of bread it always goes jam-side down. And like as not it falls where the cat's been sick into the bargain. Well, it's the way you are, isn't it? No good worrying. I mean, I wish I was more like Gwen. She's me elder sister. And what an example. Her room's not in a state like this. She's on top of things, you know what I mean? Of course she's older than me. She's always been older. I think she got the organizational ability. It had all been used up before I came along. Thank heavens there was still a bit left in one or two other departments.
    [*She heaves her large breasts.*]
You lose some, you win some, eh? That's how it is.

And I have some lovely moments to look back on, even if the snaps of them *are* all stuck together. They can't take your memories, can they? Mind, you have to work for them, you have to work for your memories Otherwise they're not worth remembering.

I fell on me feet a few times, though. Fell on me bum a few times, an' all. Well, you do, in my profession, it's a — oh what do they call it? — it's an occupational hazard, falling on your bum. In the profession. The important thing is to get up, after. Well, they taught you that at ADA. They gave us a terrific grounding there; and they didn't let up: eighteen months, the course.

And Gwen was so good to me over that. "Her little sister." If I wanted to dance, I was not to be denied. She'd scrimp and save,

I was to have my chance. Not that she had to. Scrimp and save. She's always done so well in business. She was the youngest what-d'you-ma-call-it on the counter in the whole of her firm. She beat all the men. She beat all the men. Without her, without her largesse, my opportunity, my big break — well, not big, the big breaks came later, my *first* break would have been denied me.

You see, as a little girl I used to take the stage. That's the newspaper. The organ of our profession. And in among the little advertisements near the back, you know, luxury apartments to let in Billingham, "Overcome your lisp in six easy lessons", by post, I discovered this competition. It was for girls aged sixteen next birthday and you had to send a photograph of yourself, in your swimming costume, and write a composition on why you thought you ought to be a dancer.

The prize was a chance to audition, at a reduced fee, for a place at ADA: that's the very celebrated dance school in Deptford. You'd never guess it was a converted warehouse unless you'd been there. It's run by this fabulously rich man who devotes his entire life to moulding young girls' futures. I mean, he has to go off and rest sometimes. But that's what he does, with wonderful dedication.

So anyway. I got my friend Tracy to take a snap of me in my swim things, a bit sideways on, you know, to show me off at my best. And I wrote this composition, on why I ought to be a dancer. Well, Dad's friend, Rupert, helped me. I think he could see into a girl's mind. Which is really remarkable 'cos he wasn't married and he didn't have any daughters or anything. But he wrote this marvellous stuff about flying through the air, and wanting to go up on point, and the glamorous feel of a silk bodice as the lights play on you.

I copied it all out in ink and sent it off in a big brown envelope I scrounged from Dad.

Imagine my high excitement when nine weeks later on headed notepaper I heard that I had won. Out of millions of girls who'd competed. I mean, I think the advert was in more papers than just *The Stage*. I was told it was in the *Exchange and Mart,* and *Dalton's Weekly* as well — they're two of the heavies.

So off I trekked to the hallowed portals of ADA in Deptford. The Abelard Dance Academy, itself. Named after the great middle-aged music teacher and saint, whose methods, I do believe, were the model for the Academy.

The other two hundred winners were there as well. And were we put through our paces! I mean, after all my years in the business I can see they were right to do it. We had to walk round for ages in our swimsuits so that they could assess our poise. I had more goose-pimples than a goose. Then the head of the health and efficiency department felt all our joints to see if they could take the strain that months of training were going to put on them. Then we had to get dressed in gymslips and dark stockings and come on and do "expressions". That was to see if we'd got emotional depth.

And last of all, it was into tights and a sweater, to do calisthenics, jumping this way and that as the directrice of movement shouted out. Kept taking you by surprise of course. I really did fall on my bum during that bit. But it didn't matter because they liked what they saw.

At the end of the day, the Principal, Mr Dickin, said it was the most outstanding clutch of auditions he had ever had the pleasure of witnessing, and they simply had to give almost everybody a place. The girl in the wheelchair didn't get in. Nor did the Siamese twins, though I hear they've done wonderfully since at synchronized swimming. No, that's not true. It's a joke. There weren't any Siamese twins. They were Malaysian. Lovely little pair. They didn't get in, though. Couldn't raise the £170 per term. Each.

That's where Gwen came in for me. I mean, I'd got nothing. Except my natural talent. Well, I was only fifteen. And Dad didn't get that much. Not as a pork butcher. Not that near the synagogue. And Gwen had got this fabulous job. On the counter at the Building Society.

She wouldn't hear of me missing out. I mean, she'd been to college in Derby and was full of qualifications, shorthand, longhand, I don't know what. And she said if Anthea wants — that's me, Anthea — if Anthea wants to launch herself on the quicksands of the arts I'll be right behind to give her a push. That's Gwen all over. Generous to a fault. And so neat with it! It's very shaming. I think I will just have another one of those.

So with Dad's blessing and some of Gwen's filthy lucre, I set off for the soft south.

Just turned sixteen I was when term started, two spare pair of clean knickers and a map of the underground and down I went. To Abelard's. ADA.

Well, it was an eye-opener I can tell you. Very exciting. All us young girls together from different backgrounds. Lots of common ones like me, and there was a very tall girl, I mean really tall, who was an Honourable, but she came from a very unhappy home. Her father had murdered someone — by mistake, he hadn't meant to. He'd meant to murder somebody else. Yes.

A lot of the girls had funny accents. But we were all bound together by one thing. Well, apart from the fact that we all must have been readers of *The Stage*. Or *Dalton's Weekly*. It was that we all loved to dance, go with the mood. Express our innermost feelings through our bodies.

It's real happiness when you know that. Just you, the rhythm, the music, flowing through you. Takes you over, you know. I mean, I don't mean being mindless, like some hooligan. But you're sort of at peace, I mean controlled and like creating, but at one with things. Sort of thing. It's nice. That's really nice.

And everyone's looking at you. And you know it. All the men are looking at you. Well, that's the attraction, isn't it?

So there I was. Mind, I had to do my best to keep myself. Gwen's assistance only went so far. And London prices even in those days were a sight more than we were used to paying. So, to find a bit extra, I used to go across the river to the main side and wait in a bar — well, more of a club, really — yes, I used to wait there. Serve the drinks at table, like. Wearing this very exotic costume. Lots of tasselly bits and furry bits. I was always dropping me tassels in the pernods when I put them down. The members didn't seem to mind. Some of them used to grab me tassels and wring them out. You know, for the laugh.

I mean, it were right sophisticated. Well, they were the top people in society. All the members were stockbrokers or company directors or real top-flight criminals. And it wasn't easy to tell them apart. I did work out a way after a bit: the ones whose suits were a bit smarter and who sort of talked quieter, they were the criminals. But they all treated me alike. They were all very nice to me. Course they didn't know I was only sixteen. I didn't let on. Well, it was against the law, they'd never have stood for it.

Yes. Happy times. That's what the place was called. They've pulled it down since. Built an open-air car park on the site. I think of it fondly. When I think of it. Well, I owe it, you know. You see, there's an old saying, I don't know if you're familiar with it: it's not what you know that counts; it's how long what you know could put them away for. I wouldn't have known that if I hadn't worked there. Larry the Bag taught me that. He was called Larry the Bag because his speciality was snatching handbags. Not in the club, you understand. Only when he was out, it was his profession. Only he wasn't terribly good at it. Got caught so often that most people knew him as Barry the Lag. But he was very philosophical. Well, he had the time for it. And I made some very useful contacts through him. Stood me in good stead when Academy days were over and I had to stand on my own two feet. Because the club world is a closed door if you're not on the inside.

I had my diploma of course, but they're not everything. And my talents. And like any dedicated artiste I didn't object to showing them off if it was going to lead somewhere. Tap, modern, double arabesques — they were my speciality — my passports to fame.

And they took me all over in the course of time. It started in a small way — well, you expect that, art school modelling, well, not so much art school, but artists' circles, meet once a month, you know, in somebody's front room in Mitcham or Northwick Park or somewhere. They used to like me because I had a sense of line, because of the training. I mean ADA paid off, the hours Mr Dickin put in on us.

And from doing the modelling, of course, you get known. Invitations would flood in now and then. Stag-nights, baby-sitting, you name it. They all help you get by till the moment when fame strikes.

I won't pretend there weren't some low times. When you mentioned an audition to someone you thought was your friend and she turned up and got the job. And times when you gave of your very, very best. Moved all the furniture out of the way at home to practise in advance, and you know when you're good, you know when it's flowing, and then the cheque that they promised to forward after never came. And some of those clubs, well they're too far to go and query the matter. Paying the fare again would more than use up your fee.

Still, you're building up your public, that's how I used to look at it. It's all credits, even when you're in debt.

And gradually I built up a base for myself. Moved out of the hostel and managed to rent a room for myself over the kebab shop at the top of St Martin's Lane just before you get to the Shaftesbury. Only a small room, and a bit sticky. The traffic could keep you awake unless you were very tired. But it had a great advantage if you were starving and out of funds: all you had to do was open the window at the front — well, it was the only window that did open — and put your nose out. You could smell all the cooking below. And after a couple of moments your appetite had entirely left you.

And it was dead handy being there. Friends could look in easily. People on double-decker buses looked in all the time. And when my career began to take off, thanks to Larry's introductions and one or two others, Les and Monty, I was very well placed, geographically. A number of the smaller entertainment venues were just down the road in Soho. There was the big post office by Trafalgar Square. And an all-night chemists just round the corner.

Of course, I kept in touch with the family; with Gwen, with Dad until his tragically early end, though I like to think he died fulfilled, and just a little bit proud of his younger daughter; and with Old Auntie Mabel, who I hadn't seen since I was five, but bless her, she always sent a half-crown postal order every Christmas. Even after we'd decimalized. I think she'd bought a lot in, wholesale. Well, I didn't want them to miss out on the excitement that was befalling me.

And sometimes, I admit, when things were quiet, I invented the occasional job, told them I was the one bringing on Schnozzle Durante's hat in the Royal Command Variety Show, or that I was dancing with Frankie Vaughan on his new record, things like that. Well, I didn't want them to worry. I wanted to be the colour in their lives, not the greyness.

Then one day I was doing my rather popular, though I say it myself, speciality number in a tiger skin — mock, it wasn't real — gloves with little claws stuck on, high heels, which really cost — from Freeman Hardy and Willis; in this nightclub it was, gone now, over towards Harringay. And after I'd done the number, to rapturous applause, I was quietly sipping a drink and this man came over. Said he was a professor at an American university and that he was looking for creative artists to come over and provide the occasional cultural evening. I thought well, I mustn't look too eager, so I said, casual-like, America's a long way to go.

Oh, it's not in America, he said, it's in Beirut. Well, this was the nineteen-sixties, I was only young then and I didn't know there were two Beiruts. I thought there was only the one, in South Germany. Where they do a lot of opera where Hitler used to go. I read about it in a series of learned articles entitled "Know your Dictators" in a magazine Gwen always used to take, called

Readers' Digest. So I said, oh that's not so far. So, a drink or two later he said, does that mean you'd consider it? Well, I said, I'm always looking to forward my career. It depends on the details of the offer.

He then said he thought it would be a good idea to strike while the iron was hot and to return to his hotel and discuss these very details.

I had some idea of the way things were going, but he had a nice American twang and I thought, why not? "In for a penny, in for a dollar." I mean, I'd been with boys before. Not at the Academy. The boys there were very intent on their work, and they used to worry about each other — it was a lesson to the rest of us: the older boys were always giving the younger ones a helping hand, and they just didn't seem to have spare time for enjoying themselves outside like.

But when I was home here in Duffield and on a handful of other occasions . . .

    [*She quickly counts her fingers.*]

. . . just over a handful, later, I made up for lost time. So I decided keeping this chap happy was a sacrifice I must make for my career.

Professor "Chuck" and I went off to his hotel, quite nice it was, carpet on the stairs. The receptionist greeted me as Mrs Kopanski, which was a surprise. Chuck explained he booked in as a married couple because he hated our little English breakfasts and that way he got two, which made up.

Later, when we were getting ready for bed, I asked him if everything American was bigger than here. He said it was.

    [*Brief pause.*]

But it wasn't.

Still, he was very sweet and he had a very nicely proportioned bank balance. So after a number of similar discussions, mostly in hotels along the Cromwell Road, and once or twice in my room, though he said the baby elephants on the wallpaper put him off his stride a bit, I agreed to go out to this American University in southern Germany. As I understood it.

Well, when we got there I thought what a lovely spell of weather they're having. Mind, I was surprised because I hadn't realized how much of southern Germany was by the sea; or how dark-skinned the Germans were.

Anyway, I kept my thoughts to myself because I didn't want to upset anyone.

On the second day Chuck took me to where these cultural entertainments were to be held. It looked remarkably like some of the places I'd played back home. Higher ceilings perhaps, and some roundy arches; but there was a stage against one wall with lots of shiny material draped round and behind it, and some lights; tables and chairs set round the room; and everywhere the smell of cigarette ash.

When I asked which bit of the University it was Chuck explained it wasn't actually part of the University, but they owned the premises and he rented it from them.

Then he showed me where I'd be dancing — which being a pro I'd already realized would be on the stage. He said there'd be a snake-charmer up there as well, raising his snake. And I'd be dancing to the tunes he was piping. I asked, why the snake-charmer, was he on some kind of a cultural visit, too, from the Arts Council or something? And Chuck said, no, he was local and the reason for putting us together was to show East meeting West in happy harmony.

That's when I began to realize there was more than one Beirut and this wasn't the one in Germany. Oh no, Chuck said, we're in the Lebanon, near Syria and Israel and places, this is the golden land. Funnily enough, he'd never heard of the Beirut in Germany which goes to show there are some gaps in American education. Mind, I don't think he was an avid reader, though he'd picked up a bit of French somewhere. He told me that the place was called the Café des Fleurs de Nuit de Liban. That means the Café of the Flowers of the Night of the Lebanon. Isn't that nice? Really poetic. Chuck had chosen the name himself, which I thought showed a lot of sophistication for somebody his size.

I have to admit the show itself was a great success. The undergraduates who came to see it were surprisingly old and they quite often came two or three times a week so I don't know when they did their lessons. Maybe they were all studying Western dance or something, I don't know.

And Ali was great. He was the snake-charmer – and what a charmer he was. Oh, I danced to his tune anyday. Well, he was naturally creative, you know. We met on a spiritual plane, a purely artistic plane. I mean, there was no need for speech. Well, we couldn't: he only had Arabic. Sounded like a steam locomotive pulling out of Sheffield when he ordered his breakfast. Just the same, we rubbed along famously, and in time we picked up enough words from each other to get by. We decided to form a double act. Not that we weren't already, but to stay that way, and maybe conquer the world.

I mean, I had visions of the Palladium show. You know, on the telly on Sunday night, clinging on to one of those big letters, going round and round on the revolve, waving. Ali waving, me waving, the snake . . . looking. But it wasn't to be.

Well, you can't have everything as Mam used to say before she was took.

We made it to one or two places, though, no one can deny us that. We did what we used to call the Mecca circuit: Haifa, Amman, Port Said, and of course, Mecca. Actually Ali did Mecca on his own, I just held the basket, 'cos they're funny about women there — well, they're religious you know, they can only drink and enjoy themselves when they're abroad. No, it's true. That's why they're all over here in England trying to buy up Selfridges. It's the only bit of fun they get. The pay was good though. When it finally came.

Where else did we go? We had some good dates at the Club Méditerranée in Sousse. And I suppose the highspot was the Casino, Marrakech. Admittedly, warming the snakes up was tricky because the only dressing room was miles from the performance area. We were always worried they'd go off the boil on the long walk back. Not that they walked. They were carried. But we managed.

And the standard of the show was excellent. Excellent. Very, very folklorique — see, I picked up some of the language. You can't help it when you're an international performer. Look at those opera singers. They can order chicken and chips in any language. And they do by the look of them. Oh, that reminds me.

[*She ferrets out a dirty milk bottle from under several items.*]

Must put that out for the morning. Wonder if Gwen's got any in the fridge. Hope so. Must have a look in a minute. Mind, she should be in fairly soon.

[*She checks her watch.*]

Oh, and I mustn't forget Roger's coming today an' all.

What was I saying? Oh yes, Marrakech. Well, we didn't think we could top that. And you've got to finish things when they're at their best, haven't you? Otherwise you only remember the disappointment that came after and that spoils it. You want to remember the heights. So Ali and I decided — in our respective languages — to call it a day. Besides, his wife's family in Byblos were starting to kick up. We'd been away a long time and I don't know that he was as good at the postcards home as I was.

So I turned a page in the personal history that I call life and took the ferry to Spain. Luckily, I knew folks there. Friends of Larry's who'd been successful. They'd got out of Britain before the ports were closed.

Not a lot of work there, not for a dancer with my background, 'cos they've got their own who do a lot of stamping, which isn't really my trademark. I picked up the odd gig. Entertaining at parties, big social occasions, you know, for someone's remarriage or because their brother had just been let out, that sort of thing.

And I had a fabulous time. Swimming in private pools. Talking about the old days, four or five years before, in Soho, recalling amusing occasions. Sipping tequilas in my bikini — no goose-pimples this time.

Basically, I think it was reaping my reward for all the years of work I'd put in. I really think that. And it suited me! Lady Duffield at play; yes, I'll say. But all good things come to an end and after I'd been there — oh — a good while, I was nearly as tanned as Ali, I met this man who was a promoter in England. He was on holiday with his secretary, and their children; and of course he was trying to get away from the pressures, soak up the sand and the sea and all of that. But he was a true entrepreneur and when we met and he spotted my talent, he couldn't resist his professional urges.

We got into conversation and I saw something of him over the next few days. The upshot of which was I returned with him, and his secretary, and Sharon and Wayne, the children, to the rain-soaked shores of England.

Gwen's always held that against me, as though I was doing something wrong, but it was an artistic decision. Nothing more or less. Millie, his secretary, and I always got along very well; she was a fun girl, too; and I came back because Jack said he could place me.

He had his own company, with his own little identity cards he used to give out. A very impressive address in Manchester, with two telephone lines. And let's face it, he spoke my language. I felt at home with him.

Not that I ever was. Not once I'd found out the Manchester address was a pub.

You see, Gwen thought it was a mistake. Well, so it was, but she thought I'd let my heart rule my head. She's never understood it wasn't that way round. It was a *professional* decision to come home. Unfortunately it was founded on false information. And that can happen to anybody. I expect John Gielgud's turned up at the wrong hall on occasion — when his agent's made a mistake over the date. I mean, that's a professional hazard.

But as I say, I think Gwen thinks there was more in it than the attraction of a contract. And Jack was a very good-looking man, it has to be said, but it was very little more than business, the whole thing. Very little more.

I'm sure, judged by Gwen's high standards, I sometimes fall short. But she is a remarkably good woman, my sister. Generous-hearted to everybody, but always very hard on herself. Pure, I think that's the word. Pure. Yes, I think she got all the self-control when it was being handed out. I don't know how she does it.

Years ago, there was this man in love with her. Nice. A little bit dull, came from Wirksworth. Now for some reason he didn't measure up. I mean, they were together for quite a time. He moved in for a bit, I think. Oh, I think so. I was away in London so they had the chance.

But he did something wrong. I don't know whether he made suggestions or what it was; travelled on the bus without paying, but somehow he failed to come up to her standards and Gwen threw him out. Gave him his marching orders.

Mind, I think part of it was she wanted to make sure there was a place for me here. Wasn't going to have her little sister crowded out. Though at that time I had no intention of coming back at all. The world was my oyster and I was about to prise it open. And let's face it, I did now and then, no one can gainsay that.

[*Brief pause.*]

They're not all they're cracked up to be, oysters.

And sadly the Manchester man didn't work out for me. The glittering promises: musicals at Preston, Margate summer season, "he was a friend of Trevor Nunn's, there might be something there." Well, some of them are like that. More fool me for believing him.

I did pick up a bit of work when I was first back. I did a musical at Harlow about the life of Bertrand Russell when one of the artists ricked her ankle in the shopping precinct and had to come out of it. Only it never went in. It was written by someone trying to be much too intellectual, in my opinion. And the Bertrand Russell was a terrible dancer.

I had a few gigs round here for a while and at one time I had a regular spot at a club in Chapeltown, Leeds. Then they turned it into a disco, and I'm a bit long in the leg for that.

I manage as best I can. Sis wouldn't let me go short. What's hers is mine, she's always been like that.

And luckily one or two of my gentleman fans are still very loyal. They come and visit me. Lovely to see them. Bring me little presents. Support when needed — in return for little kindnesses I can do them.

[*Brief pause.*]

Yes, that's the score.

[*Pause.*]

Look at this place. You wouldn't think I vacked it last week, would you? No? You'd be right.

Well, it's no good worrying, is it? Just accept what you are and get on with it, that's what I say.

Perhaps it'd look better if I took the bulb out.

[*She takes the bulb from a small lamp. Blackout.*]

Oh yes. I knew there was some reason I like the dark.

[*Music.*]

END OF ACT ONE

ACT TWO

Gwen

A nice chair. A nice rug. A magazine rack with the 'TV Times', 'Radio Times' and visibly, 'Readers' Digest', and a reproduction occasional table with a vase of flowers and maybe a bowl of pot-pourri.

GWEN *comes in. She makes a big deal out of sitting.*

Oh! That's better. Get the weight off my feet. There's something wrong with those chairs at work. They're not made for your back. Probably all right for fat people who after all *are* their own portable cushions. But they're a penance for those of us who take a little more pride in ourselves. Yes, that's better. Make myself a cup of Earl Grey in a moment.

That's if I can get to the tap over the soiled plates *she's* left piled up since yesterday. Yesterday! Since the week before Noah set sail, more like. If Sir Alexander Fleming hadn't discovered penicillin my sister would certainly have stumbled across it by now. She must be immune to everything the amount she's consumed from *under* the meal she's prepared. If Heinz spaghetti hoops on toast counts as a meal.

It's not as if she doesn't have the time. If I had the time on my hands that she has on hers, I'd be eating Gordon Blue every night. And she will cover everything with salad cream to disguise it. It's not as if I haven't told her about Hellmann's.

There you are, that's people. There's some will learn and some will not.

I'll be glad when this week's over and that's a fact.

    [*She picks up the 'Radio Times' and 'TV Times'.*]

Now what's on offer tonight? Snooker. No. Thank. You. Looking at men's bottoms and coloured balls is not my idea of an evening's entertainment.

A documentary on the sewage system in Rome. News to me that they have one. You'll not catch me eating Italian ice cream. I'm not putting anything to my lips that's spent the night in a box under some Romeo's bed.

A play by . . . oh, by *him!* That'll be a nasty piece of political propaganda masquerading as homespun drama. And people take it as gospel, of course. Though when it comes to voting they know better.

What else? Benny Hill. He shouldn't be allowed.

    [*She checks the magazine cover.*]

It's not the BBC one can't help noticing. Old films; more old films; why the television companies think we want to watch a lot of dead people cavorting . . . Looks like I'll have to be my own entertainment tonight. Nothing else for it.

I'd read, but my eyes get a bit tired by this time of day. Poring over figures and signatures, and these dreadful VDU screens. Mr Clench says they're the future. One day soon customers won't come into the office to deposit or discuss their chances. They'll "fax" themselves on to a VDU screen and we'll talk that way. Then it won't matter if it's raining. That's what Mr Clench says.

Though why he thinks he should know I'm sure I'm not sure. Two 'O' levels and an ill-fitting suit that drapes itself over his approaching beer-belly aren't the qualifications I'd look for in a Building Society manager. And his hair leaves marks on the wall where he leans back.

Still, look on the bright side. I don't have to pay for the redecorations.

It's not good for the Society's image though, grease patches on the flock. Not quite the ethos that some of us try to create. However, I'm happy with what *I'm* doing and that's the main thing.

I mean, I suppose I could have gone further. If I'd not been tied to staying in the Allestree office. If I'd gone to Bacup when the Society wanted to move me there. That might have been a step up for me on the ladder of success. But fate dealt me a different blow.

Had to stay at home. Anthea was away at her dance academy, so-called. Full of long girls like herself with faces like ponies, and a few boys who looked as though they'd just been popped out of a blancmange mould: perfectly formed in a small way, but inclined to quiver. So she was away, following her vocation, so it fell to me to be dutiful to the family. Father couldn't have afforded the rent — and the fees — without me.

I declined the Bacup posting and knuckled down to paying more than my way and making Father's life enjoyable. Keeping the house clean, shopping at Tesco's — he always used to run me — doing the washing: I don't know what he did with his collars, they were grimed.

Saturday afternoons were mine to call my own. He'd be off down his golf club, playing a round with one or two of his old friends.

I'd have a chance to wash my hair, "dust my jewels", whatever took my fancy.

That's how it went on. The office, the house, Saturday afternoons. Oh, for four or five years.

Stayed at home and looked after Father. Till he went off with a bus conductress thirty-one years his junior. She killed him. Killed him. Eight months later, dead in bed. Dead in bed! Dead *of* bed, if you ask me.

She took everything from him. His strength. The insurance money. His golf handicap shot up from when he knew her. And he stopped fancying his pigeons.

Which is all very well, but there they were in the loft. Pulling their feathers out and going to the toilet all over the rafters.

That's all very well. When he moved in with his "little bit of fluff," all red lips and sloppy buttocks she was, if anyone could blow bubble-gum to that size they'd be world champion. Disgusting. She can't have realized. Or she'd not have worn trousers all the time. All the time in public, that is.

So there we were: him gone and the detritus of his world littering our house.

    [*Pause.*]

I'll tell you this. I don't care if I never eat pigeon pie again. It tastes . . . it tastes like a rabbit that hasn't had a wash. And all those little bones play havoc with your fillings.

No laughing matter that. I gave up my holiday in 1973 to have this bridgework done. Well, I went private. After all, your mouth is your window on the world. So to speak. I mean, it's the first thing people notice about you, isn't it? It is when you're behind a counter and a bullet-proof glass screen. That and clean nails. So I didn't wish to advertize myself as down-at-heel National Health. With those sort of shiny front dentures that go into spasm on their own. You open your mouth in surprise and they're caught lying there. I always remember Mrs Parkinson for that. Poor woman. Nougat was her Waterloo. Two little fangs locked into a creamy-pinky blob, like a terrier with a velvet cushion. And her smiling like a set of goalposts. I wasn't having that. Oh no.

So I sacrificed Benidorm 1973. I suppose I could have still managed Blackpool for a week, or Rhyl. But I didn't care to.

And I think I have my reward.

Better looking teeth than most babies are born with. *And* the glass by *my* bed is for drinking from.

The customers like it too. The punters, as we call them. That's the business jargon. Mr Farris used to insist we called them clients. But times change. Attitudes change. And we've got to keep up. No, I think they like to see some well-fitting teeth, all in place; it helps them feel their money's secure.

Though the way some of them keep their books, you wonder if they worry about anything at all.

We had a woman the other day. Fluid Gold account. That's one up on the Daisy Chain account where you pay in every week but only a small total; I think it's for children really and young adults. Young punters. And it's not as good — in interest rate terms — as a Burnished Nugget account. That's for people who can easily afford to go private: a minimum total of ten thousand pounds in their account at all times. They're the backbone of the Society. Well worth their extra point seven five per cent. Per ann. If they all pulled out in a hurry we in the Belper and Nelson would have our problems. That's why they have to give six months' notice. Even if they die. Gives us the chance to build up elsewhere. And if all fails, gives us time to take to the lifeboat.

  [*She laughs.*]
You've got to laugh about it.

Anyway, this woman was no Burnished Nugget. She was a Fluid Gold, minimum investment, two thousand five hundred, instant withdrawal of any sum above that. Little green book with a dripping tap embossed on the front. Goldleaf naturally. Well, the dripping tap is our "logo" as we call it. The sign that means it's the Belper and Nelson for people who can't read. Not that I think we appeal much to that class of person. But it's quite witty in its way, the logo. Because Nelson is known for its water. Nelson and Colne water has filled many a bath at bathtime, and many a kettle. And Belper has its own brewery. Beer on tap, so to speak though when a certain Minister was the sitting member one might have been forgiven for thinking it was whisky that was on tap. But I don't doubt he supported the local industry as well. Anyway, he's gone to his reward. Just hope he wasn't breath-tested on the way.

So here was this woman, wearing a woollen mix overcoat that hadn't seen a brush this side of Christmas, footling about in her handbag.

I waited patiently. I could see the queue forming but I contained myself in patience; while she decorated the front of my counter with items that might better have been kept to herself: Kleenex hankies, not all of them unused; a fingerstall; a clump of keys, papers and a purse; a comb.

[*She winces.*]

A Post Office savings book which I should think went back to George VI, bless him. A bus pass, which she must have lied to get, she didn't look a day over fifty. A worn, rather raddled fifty, but fifty just the same. Unless she was minding it for her mother. Perhaps she was — should always think the best. Then out came some share certificates, a driving licence. Toilet requisites.

I mean, this went on. People in the queue were beginning to shift their weight.

A neon-coloured hairnet. Some string. A British Rail timetable. For what use that is to man or beast.

One or two people were coughing. Not me, of course, I was giving her the welcome smile. Which all we older members of the staff had been taught to do in the grounding course, which everyone used to get when we had the Barnoldswick Training Centre, before you could be let loose on the counter.

The last thing she produced, the last straw you might say, was an African National Congress tee-shirt. From her handbag. I suppose she used it as a duster, I don't know.

The man behind turned black with anger. If I remember rightly he was a Burnished Nugget. Very nice hand-sewn jacket. He'd been waiting minutes, while this woman set up a bric-a-brac stall on the counter in front of my till if you please.

Even Mr Clench noticed something was amiss. Stopped picking his spots and tapping the keys of that wretched computer to ask if I needed a hand.

I let the smile go at that point. "Not so much a hand," I called back, "more of a dumper truck." Then I smiled again, to show it was only a jest. Then the stupid woman caught her handbag with her elbow and sent several items flying on to the floor. Which was a blessing in disguise really. It gave some of the queue something to do, picking them up. Eased the mounting tension. And it released her Fluid Gold investment book from the clutches of the bus pass wallet which had previously secreted it. So I was able to complete the transaction she required, without further ado.

And people say we don't see life!

[*She gets up and starts towards the door.*]
I think I'll just get myself a cup of tea, "the cup that cheers." Though I must confess the only hooray I've heard is from me as I sip it. Oh no, we see life all right.
[*She stops by the door.*]
Naturally. All manner of persons come into a Building Society office. Not the poor and needy, of course. They'd have nothing to invest. Anyway, one can see quite enough of them down at the bus station. Why they choose to sleep there, I don't know. It's not as if they're going anywhere. And it's so draughty and smelly. There's no accounting for other people's taste.

That still leaves a wide variety. Old people using their accounts to save up for a holiday or a new gas stove. Little students trying to put a bit by so that eventually they've amassed the deposit for a flat or a starter home. I like to see that. That there are still some responsible ones being bred. There's too much easy come and easy go in my view.

That's the advantage of being on the counter, I suppose.
[*She sits.*]
If I'd had the promotion I might have been stuck in some dreary regional office, just seeing the same few faces every day. Yes, look on the bright side. I've seen more than most. I was the youngest clerk in the history of the Belper and Nelson Building Society to have her own till. It's a record that's not been beaten yet. So there's a few hundred, a few thousand clients who've been through my hands. Punters.

Oh, housewives, businessmen. People on the up. People down on their uppers. Manual workers. Menial workers. Management. A bishop at one time I remember, which I suppose counts as senior management. Florists and grocers; schoolteachers: they don't usually have much to show; Alderman Mrs Potts, she was with us. As wide a variety as you could wish for.

I'd have missed all that if I hadn't been passed over. Though if I'd been made manager of my own office I could have seen it at closer quarters. It would have been me doing the personal interviews.

"Tell me, Miss Plaskett, why you tried to withdraw fifty pounds from your account when records show you have only seventeen pounds, 57 pence in there?"

"There are a range of options open to you, Mr Woolgar. Do please study our literature and feel free to call in when you've come to a decision."

"The good news is, that your mortgage has been approved. Sir Richard."

I think I'd have been able to carry it off. With more charm than Mr Clench, though I say it myself.

Unfortunately it was not to be. Anthea was to be afforded the opportunities she wanted, so sacrifices had to be made. That's the balance of nature. I'd had to make do with a secretarial course at the Tech. and then find my own way. No money wasted on tutus and leotards for me. Not that I'd have wanted it. Too practical by far, me. No, no, I'm well content to breast the waves of commerce and leave the halls of artistic fame to others. Though I confess to a little chagrin when *they* waste their opportunities after the rest of us . . . well, never mind. No point in crying over unopened milk.

[*Brief pause.*]

Interest is due at the end of the month. In the old days we'd have spent nights working it out and then days sending out notifications. Now that's all done at Head Office. Not that anyone there actually does it. It's all in the hands of the computer. Whenever a customer happens to come in you show their book to the printer and key in the code and their interest payments are brought up to date.

One old gentleman came in not so long ago and he hadn't been near for years. Not since the Silver Jubilee, I do believe. He'd still got one of the old books. The blue design with the red corner. Well, the computer had a field day bringing him up to date, item by item. It filled over a page. I thought the thing would never stop chattering. When I finally got his book out the grand total of his interest wasn't much more than a pound. Well, he'd only had one pound, eleven pee in originally. And a new rule had come in meantime. No account to have less than five pounds in it. On any account. So we totted up his interest, gave him that and his investment and closed him down. I think he went out and bought a packet of cigarettes with it.

It was a comfort that I had not given up the last evening working all the figures out.

As I say, that's how it was in the old days. Social life went out the window in late March and September. And there was no talk of overtime payments. Oh no. You don't like the hours, you can find yourself another position. That was the attitude then. Well, it's coming back, now that unemployment's making its contribution.

But, do you know, even now people jump to the conclusion that because the office is open 9.30 am to five, those are the hours we work. It does make me laugh. Don't they realize we have to prepare a float, warm the machines up, change the date on the wall calendar, replace the stolen pens? I'm in by nine o'clock, on the dot, every morning. And many's the day I fail to make the twelve minutes past bus coming home. And it's only two steps from the office. That means waiting for the thirty-four and well gone six before I'm putting the key in my own front door. Like tonight. It's a long day when you've left at eight-fifteen in the morning. Especially when it's dark.

Doesn't leave much energy for the social life. Not at my age. Oh, I know I look good. I take care. Doesn't mean you don't feel the strain.

 [*Pause.*]

Yes, I think that was the root cause.

 [*Another pause.*]

By the time I had the time, a little bit of the fun had gone out of me.

I think that's what Reginald found.

He was very patient at first. Father was still around when Reggie and I originally met. In Maynard's sweetshop. A mix-up over some barley-sugars. He realized my time wasn't quite my own and contented himself with lunchtimes and Saturday afternoons. The ones when the Rams were playing away.

It did limit what we could share.

Sandwiches together in the churchyard by the Centre there could be very draughty, on many days of the year. Still, we were young and hardy. Sometimes there were lectures in the Municipal Art Gallery. Not that it was much warmer in there. And to be honest, I've never been a great one for Municipal Art. But it made a change.

And pre-marital holidays weren't quite the vogue in those days that they seem to be now. Well, its pre-marital marriages now, isn't it?

So we managed along. Best we could. I did a bit of darning for him. Sewed on the odd button.

And when Father decided to plough a new furrow and left me with all the worries he didn't wish to take with him, to add to the ones he'd already provided me with, Reggie was quite a support. He did the re-addressing of Father's mail, because I found that rather upsetting.

Used to come round in the evenings. Since I was free of boiled-cod-and-Horlicks duty. We had some fun times. He was always very kind.

There was one occasion, I must admit, when I allowed my emotions to get the better of me, and I encouraged him to take his pleasure. It was an extraordinary experience, though it's not something you'd want to talk about. But I don't think I'd have missed it.

And afterwards, when Reginald was lying there, a bit out of breath, he summoned himself to say, "That beat suet pudding with syrup, hands down." Lovely manners. Just goes to show.

He did a bit in the garden, too.

Helped with the pigeons.

I don't think he enjoyed wringing their necks any more than I did. Oh, and the plucking! The plucking went on for days. Feathers everywhere. I was still finding them weeks later. Under the sink. Behind the fridge. Some of them even blew through into this room. Heaven knows how.

Then as time went by, with Father gone, at work all day, nothing much to come back to at night, apart from news of madam and her goings-on, I lost a bit of my zest. It went out of me. I think it did with Reggie, too. I think maybe he found his responsibilities at Associated Tyres took their toll. At any rate our get-togethers tailed off. Petered out.

And I was left free to get on with my own life. Which I do. Be glad when this week's over though.

Holiday'll be a bit nearer then.

I've joined this club for people aged . . . well, let's say it's not the eighteen-to-thirty club. It's for people a little more mature. Interested in cultured things: Greek food, bulbfields, that sort of thing.

I've put down for this coach trip through Shakespeariana. It takes you up to Macduff's castle in the kingdom of Fife. It's in ruins now. The castle, not Fife. And then to Ware, where the great bed of Ware was in Shakespeare's day. Of course, it's not there now. The bed. Ware is. Ware's where it's always been. In Hertfordshire. Then there's a morning walking round Southwark where the Globe theatre was and after that we spend a day in Stratford, visiting the tomb, having a bite at the Judith Shakespeare Wimpy Bar and crowned by a performance by the Shakespeare actors of an African play performed in a tin hut called the Other Place.

I suppose it's called that to differentiate from somewhere called the Place. Wherever that is. Can't say I've heard of it myself. I've missed things out. It's a full week.

I'm looking forward to that. There might be some congenial company. I got on to it through one of the magazines I take. It's a chance to re-charge the batteries.

Which reminds me, I must put the kettle on.

> [*She starts to move out.*]

I suppose there'll be open tins and potato pancakes all over the draining board.

[*off*] Oh well, at least there's water in the kettle. I'll just plug it in.

ANTHEA'S VOICE:
Is that you, Sis? [*louder*] Is that you, Sis?

GWEN:
Who do you think it is, the cat's grand-daughter? Of course it's me.

ANTHEA'S VOICE:
Are you making tea in there? Is that what you're doing? Making tea? Because if you are, keep us in mind, there's a duck.

> [GWEN *appears in the doorway.* ANTHEA *continues uninterrupted.*]

Dying for a cuppa. I put water in the kettle and I wiped the cups out. And isn't it clean? Don't you think it's clean? You see, I'm a good girl sometimes. But they say one good turn deserves another, so make us some tea, pet.

GWEN:
Oh, Anthea, don't go on. I'll make your wretched tea for you.

ANTHEA'S VOICE:
Two cups, love.

GWEN:
But it'll be Earl Grey. *Two* cups! Did you say *two* cups? Have you got a man in there again? You know your trouble, my girl. You want to keep your eyes open and think of England less!

Well.

That's how it is. That's how it's always been. Firstborn I may be. Last considered. *She* has to go to dancing school. *She* has to have new dresses. Gwen'll make a contribution. Help her little sister. She's got to have her photo took for the passport. She's off to foreign climes. Gwenny'll stay at home. *She's* away making glamorous friends. Oh, look at the snaps, what a wonderful tan she's got. She *is* getting on well. She's very much in demand. Some people wanted to promote me too, but that didn't suit. Daddy needed me. Just where I was. Oh, she's sent a clipping, her name's in the paper — though how anybody knew — it was all written in Arab squiggles. She's off to another country now, a new show. She's the toast of the West End.

And what about me? The youngest teller in the history of the Belper and Nelson? I can't even move two cities away. Nobody seemed bothered whether I could sing or write poetry, or do anything. I could have got somewhere if I'd been allowed to take my chances.

Instead of which I'm saddled with *her*. When her dream career was over and Father had rutted himself into the grave she wanted to come back to "her roots". Fifty per cent of the house is hers, so I didn't have any choice. So back she came. Looking rather the worse for wear, I thought. And bringing her "dancer's" code of practice with her: laying in bed all day; indulging herself, loose relationships. Dancer! Dancer, my foot! Dancing to her was just another chance to open her legs.

Of course, it was too late for me then. My opportunity had gone to someone else. Passed me by. Not that I'm bitter. No profit in being bitter. But I must be allowed my regrets.

When it came to the abortion I point-blank refused. "Oh, but I need money for it." — "Where's all the money you've earned, our great international star?" — "Gone." — "Well, if you knew how to get rid of that, you'd better get rid of the baby in the same way."

Might have been my little niece. My little nephew.

I was that angry. I never had the chance.

She found someone to give her the money. She always does. Fans, she calls them. I know a better word for it.

There we are. That's the way of it.

I manage to have a good time in my own way. Despite everything. And I suppose I shouldn't blame her. After all, she is my own sister. You'd think, though, she could make a cup of tea for herself and whatever ageing Lothario she's practising limbo-dancing with this time — wouldn't you? I mean, it's not asking a lot, is it, to excuse your elder sister from being some kind of brothel housemaid, straightening the sheets, serving the tea — oh my God — the kettle.

    [*She dashes off.*]

[*off*] Oh no. Oh, I don't believe it. It was only new from Comet a few months ago. Oh well, that's it. Anthea! Anthea! There's no tea. The kettle's burnt itself out.

[*She appears and crosses the room, carrying a glass.*]
Burnt itself right out. The element's gone. So if you want anything to drink, it'll have to be water from the tap.

[*She gets out a bottle of whisky and pours some in the glass.*]
Sorry love. There's nothing else.

[*The lights go down.*]

THE END